TONBRIDGE SCHOOL POUND

(BLOCK CAPITALS)	FORM OR SET	DATE OF ISSUE	MASTER'S INITIALS
Edward Brash	AE2	19/1/93	

THE LESS DECEIVED

THE LESS DECEIVED

Poems

by

PHILIP LARKIN

THE MARVELL PRESS

First published in October 1955
by
The Marvell Press
First published in this edition 1977
All rights reserved
Reprinted 1985/1988/1991

Printed and bound by
Woolnough Bookbinding Ltd, Irthlingborough, Northants

Acknowledgments are due to the editors of *Departure, Listen, The Listener, Platform, Poetry and Audience, Shenandoah, The Spectator,* in whose pages some of these poems have previously appeared. Others have been broadcast on the B.B.C. Third Programme. Five were published in *Springtime* (Peter Owen, 1953), and five in *Fantasy Press : Pamphlet* 21 (1954).

CONTENTS

To
Monica Jones

LINES ON A YOUNG LADY'S
PHOTOGRAPH ALBUM

At last you yielded up the album, which,
Once open, sent me distracted. All your ages
Matt and glossy on the thick black pages!
Too much confectionery, too rich:
I choke on such nutritious images.

My swivel eye hungers from pose to pose —
In pigtails, clutching a reluctant cat;
Or furred yourself, a sweet girl-graduate;
Or lifting a heavy-headed rose
Beneath a trellis, or in a trilby hat

(Faintly disturbing, that, in several ways) —
From every side you strike at my control,
Not least through these disquieting chaps who loll
At ease about your earlier days:
Not quite your class, I'd say, dear, on the whole.

But o, photography! as no art is,
Faithful and disappointing! that records
Dull days as dull, and hold-it smiles as frauds,
And will not censor blemishes
Like washing-lines, and Hall's-Distemper boards,

But shows the cat as disinclined, and shades
A chin as doubled when it is, what grace
Your candour thus confers upon her face!
How overwhelmingly persuades
That this is a real girl in a real place,

In every sense empirically true!
Or is it just *the past*? Those flowers, that gate,
These misty parks and motors, lacerate
Simply by being over; you
Contract my heart by looking out of date.

Yes, true; but in the end, surely, we cry
Not only at exclusion, but because
It leaves us free to cry. We know *what was*
Won't call on us to justify
Our grief, however hard we yowl across

The gap from eye to page. So I am left
To mourn (without a chance of consequence)
You, balanced on a bike against a fence;
To wonder if you'd spot the theft
Of this one of you bathing; to condense,

In short, a past that no one now can share,
No matter whose your future; calm and dry,
It holds you like a heaven, and you lie
Unvariably lovely there,
Smaller and clearer as the years go by.

WEDDING-WIND

The wind blew all my wedding-day,
And my wedding-night was the night of the high wind;
And a stable door was banging, again and again,
That he must go and shut it, leaving me
Stupid in candlelight, hearing rain,
Seeing my face in the twisted candlestick,
Yet seeing nothing. When he came back
He said the horses were restless, and I was sad
That any man or beast that night should lack
The happiness I had.

              Now in the day
All's ravelled under the sun by the wind's blowing.
He has gone to look at the floods, and I
Carry a chipped pail to the chicken-run,
Set it down, and stare. All is the wind
Hunting through clouds and forests, thrashing
My apron and the hanging cloths on the line.
Can it be borne, this bodying-forth by wind
Of joy my actions turn on, like a thread
Carrying beads? Shall I be let to sleep
Now this perpetual morning shares my bed?
Can even death dry up
These new delighted lakes, conclude
Our kneeling as cattle by all-generous waters?

PLACES, LOVED ONES

No, I have never found
The place where I could say
This is my proper ground,
Here I shall stay;
Nor met that special one
Who has an instant claim
On everything I own
Down to my name;

To find such seems to prove
You want no choice in where
To build, or whom to love;
You ask them to bear
You off irrevocably,
So that it's not your fault
Should the town turn dreary,
The girl a dolt. .

Yet, having missed them, you're
Bound, none the less, to act
As if what you settled for
Mashed you, in fact;
And wiser to keep away
From thinking you still might trace
Uncalled-for to this day
Your person, your place.

COMING

On longer evenings,
Light, chill and yellow,
Bathes the serene
Foreheads of houses.
A thrush sings,
Laurel-surrounded
In the deep bare garden,
Its fresh-peeled voice
Astonishing the brickwork.
It will be spring soon,
It will be spring soon —
And I, whose childhood
Is a forgotten boredom,
Feel like a child
Who comes on a scene
Of adult reconciling,
And can understand nothing
But the unusual laughter,
And starts to be happy.

REASONS FOR ATTENDANCE

The trumpet's voice, loud and authoritative,
Draws me a moment to the lighted glass
To watch the dancers — all under twenty-five —
Shifting intently, face to flushed face,
Solemnly on the beat of happiness.

— Or so I fancy, sensing the smoke and sweat,
The wonderful feel of girls. Why be out here?
But then, why be in there? Sex, yes, but what
Is sex? Surely, to think the lion's share
Of happiness is found by couples — sheer

Inaccuracy, as far as I'm concerned.
What calls me is that lifted, rough-tongued bell
(Art, if you like) whose individual sound
Insists I too am individual.
It speaks; I hear; others may hear as well,

But not for me, nor I for them; and so
With happiness. Therefore I stay outside,
Believing this; and they maul to and fro,
Believing that; and both are satisfied,
If no one has misjudged himself. Or lied.

DRY-POINT

Endlessly, time-honoured irritant,
A bubble is restively forming at your tip.
Burst it as fast as we can —
It will grow again, until we begin dying.

Silently it inflates, till we're enclosed
And forced to start the struggle to get out :
Bestial, intent, real.
The wet spark comes, the bright blown walls collapse,

But what sad scapes we cannot turn from then :
What ashen hills ! what salted, shrunken lakes !
How leaden the ring looks,
Birmingham magic all discredited,

And how remote that bare and sunscrubbed room,
Intensely far, that padlocked cube of light
We neither define nor prove,
Where you, we dream, obtain no right of entry.

NEXT, PLEASE

Always too eager for the future, we
Pick up bad habits of expectancy.
Something is always approaching; every day
Till then we say,

Watching from a bluff the tiny, clear,
Sparkling armada of promises draw near.
How slow they are! And how much time they waste,
Refusing to make haste!

Yet still they leave us holding wretched stalks
Of disappointment, for, though nothing balks
Each big approach, leaning with brasswork prinked,
Each rope distinct,

Flagged, and the figurehead with golden tits
Arching our way, it never anchors; it's
No sooner present than it turns to past.
Right to the last

We think each one will heave to and unload
All good into our lives, all we are owed
For waiting so devoutly and so long.
But we are wrong:

Only one ship is seeking us, a black-
Sailed unfamiliar, towing at her back
A huge and birdless silence. In her wake
No waters breed or break.

GOING

There is an evening coming in
Across the fields, one never seen before,
That lights no lamps.

Silken it seems at a distance, yet
When it is drawn up over the knees and breast
It brings no comfort.

Where has the tree gone, that locked
Earth to the sky? What is under my hands,
That I cannot feel?

What loads my hands down?

WANTS

Beyond all this, the wish to be alone :
However the sky grows dark with invitation-cards
However we follow the printed directions of sex
However the family is photographed under the flagstaff —
Beyond all this, the wish to be alone.

Beneath it all, desire of oblivion runs :
Despite the artful tensions of the calendar,
The life insurance, the tabled fertility rites,
The costly aversion of the eyes from death —
Beneath it all, desire of oblivion runs.

MAIDEN NAME

Marrying left your maiden name disused.
Its five light sounds no longer mean your face,
Your voice, and all your variants of grace;
For since you were so thankfully confused
By law with someone else, you cannot be
Semantically the same as that young beauty :
It was of her that these two words were used.

Now it's a phrase applicable to no one,
Lying just where you left it, scattered through
Old lists, old programmes, a school prize or two,
Packets of letters tied with tartan ribbon —
Then is it scentless, weightless, strengthless, wholly
Untruthful? Try whispering it slowly.
No, it means you. Or, since you're past and gone,

It means what we feel now about you then :
How beautiful you were, and near, and young,
So vivid, you might still be there among
Those first few days, unfingermarked again.
So your old name shelters our faithfulness,
Instead of losing shape and meaning less
With your depreciating luggage laden.

BORN YESTERDAY

for Sally Amis

Tightly-folded bud,
I have wished you something
None of the others would :
Not the usual stuff
About being beautiful,
Or running off a spring
Of innocence and love —
They will all wish you that,
And should it prove possible,
Well, you're a lucky girl.

But if it shouldn't, then
May you be ordinary;
Have, like other women,
An average of talents :
Not ugly, not good-looking,
Nothing uncustomary
To pull you off your balance,
That, unworkable itself,
Stops all the rest from working.
In fact, may you be dull —
If that is what a skilled,
Vigilant, flexible,
Unemphasised, enthralled
Catching of happiness is called.

WHATEVER HAPPENED?

At once whatever happened starts receding.
Panting, and back on board, we line the rail
With trousers ripped, light wallets, and lips bleeding.

Yes, gone, thank God! Remembering each detail
We toss for half the night, but find next day
All's kodak-distant. Easily, then (though pale),

'Perspective brings significance,' we say,
Unhooding our photometers, and, snap!
What can't be printed can be thrown away.

Later, it's just a latitude : the map
Points out how unavoidable it was :
'Such coastal bedding always means mishap.'

Curses? The dark? Struggling? Where's the source
Of these yarns now (except in nightmares, of course)?

NO ROAD

Since we agreed to let the road between us
Fall to disuse,
And bricked our gates up, planted trees to screen us,
And turned all time's eroding agents loose,
Silence, and space, and strangers — our neglect
Has not had much effect.

Leaves drift unswept, perhaps; grass creeps unmown;
No other change.
So clear it stands, so little overgrown,
Walking that way tonight would not seem strange,
And still would be allowed. A little longer,
And time will be the stronger,

Drafting a world where no such road will run
From you to me;
To watch that world come up like a cold sun,
Rewarding others, is my liberty.
Not to prevent it is my will's fulfilment.
Willing it, my ailment.

WIRES

The widest prairies have electric fences,
For though old cattle know they must not stray
Young steers are always scenting purer water
Not here but anywhere. Beyond the wires

Leads them to blunder up against the wires
Whose muscle-shredding violence gives no quarter.
Young steers become old cattle from that day,
Electric limits to their widest senses.

CHURCH GOING

Once I am sure there's nothing going on
I step inside, letting the door thud shut.
Another church : matting, seats, and stone,
And little books; sprawlings of flowers, cut
For Sunday, brownish now; some brass and stuff
Up at the holy end; the small neat organ;
And a tense, musty, unignorable silence,
Brewed God knows how long. Hatless, I take off
My cycle-clips in awkward reverence,

Move forward, run my hand around the font.
From where I stand, the roof looks almost new —
Cleaned, or restored? Someone would know : I don't.
Mounting the lectern, I peruse a few
Hectoring large-scale verses, and pronounce
'Here endeth' much more loudly than I'd meant.
The echoes snigger briefly. Back at the door
I sign the book, donate an Irish sixpence,
Reflect the place was not worth stopping for.

Yet stop I did : in fact I often do,
And always end much at a loss like this,
Wondering what to look for; wondering, too,
When churches fall completely out of use
What we shall turn them into, if we shall keep
A few cathedrals chronically on show,
Their parchment, plate and pyx in locked cases,
And let the rest rent-free to rain and sheep.
Shall we avoid them as unlucky places?

Or, after dark, will dubious women come
To make their children touch a particular stone;
Pick simples for a cancer; or on some
Advised night see walking a dead one?
Power of some sort or other will go on
In games, in riddles, seemingly at random;
But superstition, like belief, must die,
And what remains when disbelief has gone?
Grass, weedy pavement, brambles, buttress, sky,

A shape less recognisable each week,
A purpose more obscure. I wonder who
Will be the last, the very last, to seek
This place for what it was; one of the crew
That tap and jot and know what rood-lofts were?
Some ruin-bibber, randy for antique,
Or Christmas-addict, counting on a whiff
Of gowns-and-bands and organ-pipes and myrrh?
Or will he be my representative,

Bored, uninformed, knowing the ghostly silt
Dispersed, yet tending to this cross of ground
Through suburb scrub because it held unspilt
So long and equably what since is found
Only in separation — marriage, and birth,
And death, and thoughts of these — for which was built
This special shell? For, though I've no idea
What this accoutred frowsty barn is worth,
It pleases me to stand in silence here;

A serious house on serious earth it is,
In whose blent air all our compulsions meet,
Are recognised, and robed as destinies.
And that much never can be obsolete,
Since someone will forever be surprising
A hunger in himself to be more serious,
And gravitating with it to this ground,
Which, he once heard, was proper to grow wise in,
If only that so many dead lie round.

AGE

My age fallen away like white swaddling
Floats in the middle distance, becomes
An inhabited cloud. I bend closer, discern
A lighted tenement scuttling with voices.
O you tall game I tired myself with joining!
Now I wade through you like knee-level weeds,

And they attend me, dear translucent bergs:
Silence and space. By now so much has flown
From the nest here of my head that I needs must turn
To know what prints I leave, whether of feet,
Or spoor of pads, or a bird's adept splay.

MYXOMATOSIS

Caught in the centre of a soundless field
While hot inexplicable hours go by
What trap is this? Where were its teeth concealed?
You seem to ask.
                I make a sharp reply,
Then clean my stick. I'm glad I can't explain
Just in what jaws you were to suppurate :
You may have thought things would come right again
If you could only keep quite still and wait.

TOADS

Why should I let the toad *work*
   Squat on my life?
Can't I use my wit as a pitchfork
   And drive the brute off?

Six days of the week it soils
   With its sickening poison —
Just for paying a few bills!
   That's out of proportion.

Lots of folk live on their wits:
   Lecturers, lispers,
Losels, loblolly-men, louts —
   They don't end as paupers;

Lots of folk live up lanes
   With fires in a bucket,
Eat windfalls and tinned sardines —
   They seem to like it.

Their nippers have got bare feet,
   Their unspeakable wives
Are skinny as whippets — and yet
   No one actually *starves*.

Ah, were I courageous enough
   To shout *Stuff your pension!*
But I know, all too well, that's the stuff
   That dreams are made on:

For something sufficiently toad-like
   Squats in me, too;
Its hunkers are heavy as hard luck,
   And cold as snow,

And will never allow me to blarney
   My way to getting
The fame and the girl and the money
   All at one sitting.

I don't say, one bodies the other
   One's spiritual truth;
But I do say it's hard to lose either,
   When you have both.

POETRY OF DEPARTURES

Sometimes you hear, fifth-hand,
As epitaph :
He chucked up everything
And just cleared off,
And always the voice will sound
Certain you approve
This audacious, purifying,
Elemental move.

And they are right, I think.
We all hate home
And having to be there :
I detest my room,
Its specially-chosen junk,
The good books, the good bed,
And my life, in perfect order :
So to hear it said

He walked out on the whole crowd
Leaves me flushed and stirred,
Like *Then she undid her dress*
Or *Take that you bastard*;
Surely I can, if he did?
And that helps me stay
Sober and industrious.
But I'd go today,

Yes, swagger the nut-strewn roads,
Crouch in the fo'c'sle
Stubbly with goodness, if
It weren't so artificial,
Such a deliberate step backwards
To create an object :
Books; china; a life
Reprehensibly perfect.

TRIPLE TIME

This empty street, this sky to blandness scoured,
This air, a little indistinct with autumn
Like a reflection, constitute the present —
A time traditionally soured,
A time unrecommended by event.

But equally they make up something else :
This is the future furthest childhood saw
Between long houses, under travelling skies,
Heard in contending bells —
An air lambent with adult enterprise,

And on another day will be the past,
A valley cropped by fat neglected chances
That we insensately forbore to fleece.
On this we blame our last
Threadbare perspectives, seasonal decrease.

SPRING

Green-shadowed people sit, or walk in rings,
Their children finger the awakened grass,
Calmly a cloud stands, calmly a bird sings,
And, flashing like a dangled looking-glass,
Sun lights the balls that bounce, the dogs that bark,
The branch-arrested mist of leaf, and me,
Threading my pursed-up way across the park,
An indigestible sterility.

Spring, of all seasons most gratuitous,
Is fold of untaught flower, is race of water,
Is earth's most multiple, excited daughter;

And those she has least use for see her best,
Their paths grown craven and circuitous,
Their visions mountain-clear, their needs immodest.

DECEPTIONS

*'Of course I was drugged, and so heavily I did
not regain my consciousness till the next morning.
I was horrified to discover that I had been ruined,
and for some days I was inconsolable, and cried
like a child to be killed or sent back to my aunt.'*—
Mayhew, *London Labour and the London Poor.*

Even so distant, I can taste the grief,
Bitter and sharp with stalks, he made you gulp.
The sun's occasional print, the brisk brief
Worry of wheels along the street outside
Where bridal London bows the other way,
And light, unanswerable and tall and wide,
Forbids the scar to heal, and drives
Shame out of hiding. All the unhurried day
Your mind lay open like a drawer of knives.

Slums, years, have buried you. I would not dare
Console you if I could. What can be said,
Except that suffering is exact, but where
Desire takes charge, readings will grow erratic?
For you would hardly care
That you were less deceived, out on that bed,
Than he was, stumbling up the breathless stair
To burst into fulfilment's desolate attic.

I REMEMBER, I REMEMBER

Coming up England by a different line
For once, early in the cold new year,
We stopped, and, watching men with number-plates
Sprint down the platform to familiar gates,
'Why, Coventry!' I exclaimed. 'I was born here.'

I leant far out, and squinnied for a sign
That this was still the town that had been 'mine'
So long, but found I wasn't even clear
Which side was which. From where those cycle-crates
Were standing, had we annually departed

For all those family hols? . . . A whistle went :
Things moved. I sat back, staring at my boots.
'Was that,' my friend smiled, 'where you "have your roots"?'
No, only where my childhood was unspent,
I wanted to retort, just where I started :

By now I've got the whole place clearly charted.
Our garden, first : where I did not invent
Blinding theologies of flowers and fruits,
And wasn't spoken to by an old hat.
And here we have that splendid family

I never ran to when I got depressed,
The boys all biceps and the girls all chest,
Their comic Ford, their farm where I could be
'Really myself'. I'll show you, come to that,
The bracken where I never trembling sat,

Determined to go through with it; where she
Lay back, and 'all became a burning mist'.
And, in those offices, my doggerel
Was not set up in blunt ten-point, nor read
By a distinguished cousin of the mayor,

Who didn't call and tell my father *There*
Before us, had we the gift to see ahead —
'You look as if you wished the place in Hell,'
My friend said, 'judging from your face.' 'Oh well,
I suppose it's not the place's fault,' I said.

'Nothing, like something, happens anywhere.'

ABSENCES

Rain patters on a sea that tilts and sighs.
Fast-running floors, collapsing into hollows,
Tower suddenly, spray-haired. Contrariwise,
A wave drops like a wall : another follows,
Wilting and scrambling, tirelessly at play
Where there are no ships and no shallows.

Above the sea, the yet more shoreless day,
Riddled by wind, trails lit-up galleries :
They shift to giant ribbing, sift away.

Such attics cleared of me ! Such absences !

LATEST FACE

Latest face, so effortless
Your great arrival at my eyes,
No one standing near could guess
Your beauty had no home till then;
Precious vagrant, recognise
My look, and do not turn again.

Admirer and admired embrace
On a useless level, where
I contain your current grace,
You my judgment; yet to move
Into real untidy air
Brings no lasting attribute —
Bargains, suffering, and love,
Not this always-planned salute.

Lies grow dark around us : will
The statue of your beauty walk?
Must I wade behind it, till
Something's found — or is not found —
Far too late for turning back?
Or, if I will not shift my ground,
Is your power actual — can
Denial of you duck and run,
Stay out of sight and double round,
Leap from the sun with mask and brand
And murder and not understand?

IF, MY DARLING

If my darling were once to decide
Not to stop at my eyes,
But to jump, like Alice, with floating skirt into my head,

She would find no tables and chairs,
No mahogany claw-footed sideboards,
No undisturbed embers;

The tantalus would not be filled, nor the fender-seat cosy,
Nor the shelves stuffed with small-printed books for the Sabbath,
Nor the butler bibulous, the housemaids lazy :

She would find herself looped with the creep of varying light,
Monkey-brown, fish-grey, a string of infected circles
Loitering like bullies, about to coagulate;

Delusions that shrink to the size of a woman's glove
Then sicken inclusively outwards. She would also remark
The unwholesome floor, as it might be the skin of a grave,

From which ascends an adhesive sense of betrayal,
A Grecian statue kicked in the privates, money,
A swill-tub of finer feelings. But most of all

She'd be stopping her ears against the incessant recital
Intoned by reality, larded with technical terms,
Each one double-yolked with meaning and meaning's rebuttal :

For the skirl of that bulletin unpicks the world like a knot,
And to hear how the past is past and the future neuter
Might knock my darling off her unpriceable pivot.

SKIN

Obedient daily dress,
You cannot always keep
That unfakable young surface.
You must learn your lines —
Anger, amusement, sleep;
Those few forbidding signs

Of the continuous coarse
Sand-laden wind, time;
You must thicken, work loose
Into an old bag
Carrying a soiled name.
Parch then; be roughened; sag;

And pardon me, that I
Could find, when you were new,
No brash festivity
To wear you at, such as
Clothes are entitled to
Till the fashion changes.

ARRIVALS, DEPARTURES

This town has docks where channel boats come sidling;
Tame water lanes, tall sheds, the traveller sees
(His bag of samples knocking at his knees),
And hears, still under slackened engines gliding,
His advent blurted to the morning shore.

And we, barely recalled from sleep there, sense
Arrivals lowing in a doleful distance —
Horny dilemmas at the gate once more.
Come and choose wrong, they cry, *come and choose wrong;*
And so we rise. At night again they sound,

Calling the traveller now, the outward bound :
O not for long, they cry, *O not for long —*
And we are nudged from comfort, never knowing
How safely we may disregard their blowing,
Or if, this night, happiness too is going.

AT GRASS

The eye can hardly pick them out
From the cold shade they shelter in,
Till wind distresses tail and mane;
Then one crops grass, and moves about
— The other seeming to look on —
And stands anonymous again.

Yet fifteen years ago, perhaps
Two dozen distances sufficed
To fable them : faint afternoons
Of Cups and Stakes and Handicaps,
Whereby their names were artificed
To inlay faded, classic Junes —

Silks at the start : against the sky
Numbers and parasols : outside,
Squadrons of empty cars, and heat,
And littered grass : then the long cry
Hanging unhushed till it subside
To stop-press columns on the street.

Do memories plague their ears like flies?
They shake their heads. Dusk brims the shadows.
Summer by summer all stole away,
The starting-gates, the crowds and cries —
All but the unmolesting meadows.
Almanacked, their names live; they

Have slipped their names, and stand at ease,
Or gallop for what must be joy,
And not a fieldglass sees them home,
Or curious stop-watch prophesies :
Only the groom, and the groom's boy,
With bridles in the evening come.

AN ENORMOUS YES
in memoriam Philip Larkin
(1922–1985)

PHILIP LARKIN
Two unpublished poems
Two uncollected poems
'Not The Place's Fault'
(Philip Larkin writes about his Coventry childhood)
Philip Larkin on poetry
Philip Larkin on death
Photographs

and other items from the University of Hull Larkin Exhibition

Tributes by
Peter Levi · Craig Raine · David Selzer

Poems by

Andrew Motion   William Scammell   Vernon Scannell

David Sutton   Anthony Thwaite

and others

"The inclusion of previously unpublished or uncollected pieces makes [this volume] a must for [Larkin's] admirers."
Wendy Cope/Daily Telegraph

"Poems, prose tributes, published and unpublished pieces by Philip Larkin himself, photographs and drawings make up Harry Chambers's attractive memorial."
Lachlan Mackinnon/Times Literary Supplement

"splendid tributes"
Observer/Paperback Choice

ISBN 0 905291 85 9 PETERLOO POETS   72 pages paperback

£4.95 post free (U.K.)

2 KELLY GARDENS · CALSTOCK · CORNWALL PL18 9SA · U.K.

PETERLOO POETS

'. . . a series kept up to scratch for a good few years by publisher Harry Chambers's energy and discrimination.'

Roy Fuller/Spectator

'Harry Chambers, the publisher of *Peterloo Poets*, continues to put to shame the London publishing houses, in the flow of attractively produced volumes coming from his press. The poet who finds his major outlet in the *Peterloo* series is fortunate indeed.'

D. M. Thomas/Arts South West

'I share with others an admiration for the *Peterloo Poets* imprint, particularly the way they can put the fashionable to shame and produce winners from unlikely stables.'

Brian Jones/London Magazine

'*Peterloo Poets* is a small publishing house run by Harry Chambers in Cornwall. Its books are sensitively designed; each has a striking illustrated cover and the typography is excellent. The quality of production is much better than the usual standard of poetry paperbacks issued by major publishers.'

G. B. H. Wightman/British Book News

'There's a solid consistency about the *Peterloo Poets* series . . . Design and printing are always excellent, and the poems themselves are never less than interesting, not least because they tend to be by people who've already done some living and have something to say.'

Grevel Lindop/Times Literary Supplement

Full Stocklist, including New & Forthcoming Titles (post free) from:

Peterloo Poets, 2 Kelly Gardens, Calstock, Cornwall PL18 9SA, U.K.